The Song of Malan

www.royalcollins.com

The Song of Malan

Written by Xu Lu   Illustrated by Ge Huanhuan

RC

Books Beyond Boundaries

ROYAL COLLINS

The Song of Malan

Written by Xu Lu
Illustrated by Ge Huanhuan

First published in 2024 by Royal Collins Publishing Group Inc.
Groupe Publication Royal Collins Inc.
BKM Royalcollins Publishers Private Limited

Headquarters: 550-555 boul. René-Lévesque O Montréal (Québec)
H2Z1B1 Canada
India office: 805 Hemkunt House, 8th Floor, Rajendra Place,
New Delhi 110 008

Copyright © Xu Lu, Ge Huanhuan, 2024
Original edition © Anhui Children's Publishing House Co., Ltd.
B&R Book Program

ISBN: 978-1-4878-1175-4

To find out more about our publications,
please visit www.royalcollins.com.

Foreword

The Communist Party of China fought valiantly and spilled blood for national liberation, founding the New China, all to ensure happiness and prosperity for every citizen.

My mission is to bring music to children deprived of songs, making music a lifelong companion for them.

I believe that with the company of music, these children will grow up healthier and happier and will develop a deeper love for our motherland. They will embody strength and confidence throughout their lives, living happily and fulfilled.

Deng Xiaolan
October 2019
Yongle Community, Beijing

Many songs have vanished,

but one will forever echo in my heart.

Where is that song? Does it drift among the tall mountains or under the rose-colored clouds?

Ah, thinking about it now, it seems so far away...

And yet, it is that distance that makes it even more precious.

Malan Village is a small village nestled deep in the Taihang Mountains in Fuping County, Hebei Province, north of China.

White pear blossoms and purple wisteria flowers surround the village in the spring. In the autumn, the wild chestnut and maple tree leaves on the hills turn golden, deep red, and amber under the sun. Every evening, the villagers bring their cows and sheep back to the small village from the hills when the cooking smoke rises.

During the final and heroic battle against the Japanese fascist invaders from 1931 to 1945, my father, mother, comrades, and countless Chinese people were fighting.

My father told my mother that the invaders would soon be driven out of the Taihang Mountains and out of China. Our baby was born then, bringing us the message of peace!

At that time, I was just a nursing infant lying on a *kang*, a bed and a stove that kept us warm in winter.

To show their gratitude to Malan Village, my parents named me "Xiaolanzi," meaning little orchid.

After I was born, my parents sent me to live with a family in the Malan Village. Then they shouldered their backpacks and went to the front line of the war.

I grew up daily on the *kang* in the Malan villagers' home, on the tanned back of the village elder, in the wicker basket carried by the miniature donkey, on the shoulders of my village playmates, under the old locust tree at the entrance to the village.

After winning the War of Resistance, my parents came to
Malan Village and brought me back home. In the spring
of 2004, when the wisteria flowers were in full bloom, I
returned to Malan Village again, fulfilling my parents' wish.

马兰惨案遇难同胞纪念碑

We erected a tall monument at the village entrance to commemorate the nineteen villagers of Malan killed by Japanese fascists over sixty years ago.

Standing before the monument,
I asked two children, "Do you
know how to sing the national
anthem?" They shook their
heads in silence.

How can no birds sing in the small grove at dawn and dusk? And just like the wisteria-covered village of Malan, how can there be no stream flowing softly?

The villagers of Malan have not lost their smiles and songs. I believe the warm spring will melt the glaciers and awaken the sleeping valleys and blooming azaleas.

Starting from that spring, my most significant and most beautiful dream was to bring back the lost songs of Malan Village.

After returning to Beijing, I rallied my family and friends
and raised funds to rebuild the dilapidated village school.

In the end, we were able to construct seven beautiful new classrooms for the students in the village.

Since then, I have brought various musical instruments from Beijing to Malan Village with the help of my family and friends' donations. I have become familiar with every small station and field from Beijing to Malan Village.

For the first time, the children were introduced to instruments such as the accordion, violin, guitar, and mandolin.

We formed the first small band in Malan Village.

We sang on the hill where
the reeds danced in the
wind, by the waterfall and
the mountain spring…

Distant fathers who worked away also
heard their children playing the violin.

Sometimes, adults and children would compete
to play the accordion.

And so, singing and laughing, we welcomed
the first-ever Malan Children's Music Festival.

The sky was filled with the sound of children singing.

The moonlight also carries our serenade under the night sky.

The children from the Malan Children's Music Festival were invited to perform on the stage of the Beijing Television Spring Festival Gala, the biggest event of the year and the most-watched program.

Singing and laughing, we stood on the stage of the Beijing Winter Olympics.

I know that someday, I will grow old and be unable to walk again.

But beautiful music never dies, and the songs of Malan Village will never be lost again.

They will forever be with the villagers of Malan and every generation of children.

About the Author

Xu Lu is an esteemed Chinese children's literature author and a distinguished member of the Chinese Writers Association. His former role as the vice-chairman of the Hubei Writers Association further highlights his prominence in the literary community. Xu Lu's contribution to children's literature is noteworthy, with over 20 of his works incorporated into Chinese primary and middle school language curricula. His novels, such as *Children of the Lop Nur*, *The Youth Knows All the Tastes of Sorrow*, and *For Eternity*, have garnered widespread acclaim within China's literary circles.

Several prestigious organizations have recognized and honored his literary achievements, including the National Publication Fund and the Central Publicity Department. Xu Lu's accolades include the National Excellent Children's Literature Award, the Bingxin Children's Book Award, and the Chen Bochui International Children's Literature Award.

Furthermore, Xu Lu's literary influence extends beyond Chinese borders. His works have been translated into English, German, and other languages, gaining international readership and acclaim. This global reach underscores the universal appeal and significance of his contributions to children's literature.

About the Illustrator

Ge Huanhuan is a talented artist hailing from Kaifeng, Henan Province. She received her master's degree in watercolor from the prestigious Xi'an Academy of Fine Arts. Her works have been featured in numerous provincial exhibitions, and she has received several awards for her remarkable artistic contributions. In 2017, her piece *Time Casting Poetry* was selected for display at the prestigious Today's Silk Road International Art Invitation Exhibition, sponsored by the Chinese Ministry of Culture and the Shaanxi Provincial People's Government. Ge's first picture book, *The Song of Malan*, is a stunning showcase of her artistic talent and passion for capturing the beauty and wonder of the world around us.